Something Dark to Shine In

Sundress Publications • Knoxville, TN

ISBN: 978-1-951979-25-6
Library of Congress:2021948511
Published by Sundress Publications
www.sundresspublications.com

Editor: Marci Calabretta
Editorial Assistants: Anna Black, Kanika Lawton, Erin Elizabeth Smith
Editorial Interns: Stephi Cham, Katy DeCoste, Ryleigh Wann

Colophon: This book is set in Bell MT.
Cover Image: "Mariposa" by Katie McCann
Cover Design: Kristen Ton
Book Design: Tierney Bailey

Something Dark to Shine In

Inès Pujos

ACKNOWLEDGMENTS

Many thanks from the author to the editors of the publications in which the following poems first appeared:

"Everything Hides Us," "Calvary," and "The Swallows," first appeared in *Fog Machine*.

"Self Portrait as Beast Inside Belly," first appeared in *Salt Hill Press*.

"On Becoming," and "Lily of The Valley," first appeared in *Poor Claudia*.

"The Mellified Men," first appeared in *The Journal*.

"The Two Matrons of Death," and "Young Girl Eating A Bird," first appeared in *Cosmonauts Avenue*.

"Against Porcelain," first appeared in *Gulf Coast Review*.

"More Blood in The East Village," and "How Much Whiskey Am I Supposed To Drink Before I become a Ghost," first appeared in *Powder Keg*.

"In Good Faith," first appeared in *Bone Bouquet*.

"Random Attack," first appeared in *The Adroit Journal*.

"A New Frontier," first appeared in *The Offing*.

CONTENTS

For my fellow survivors,
I believe you, you are valid.

"I'll just bleed so the stars can have something dark to shine in."

—Frank Stanford

ON BECOMING

When the family dog goes missing, you go days
without showering & coat your gums with moss,

take to comb & spray your bush
thick in artichoke. Admit it.

Fall & find him in the woods. His head now
unrecognizable, a black wool of flies sticks to him.

Bring him to the meatswap & trade his skull
for a bundle of beets, his teeth for peonies.

With machete in hand, hack open the belly
of a pregnant cow. With placenta shriveled,

you crawl inside. It's winter. There is no more light.
Strap a deer's face to your own.

Take antlers for ears.

AGAINST PORCELAIN

For Maxime, drowned August 2011

Scientists in Hong Kong have discovered a prehistoric fish
washed ashore in my bathtub among hair knots & soap suds
National Geographic is on its way
this creature with ten eyes & no fins
there are debates whether it is native
I stick my hand in the giant tub & when I don't feel
any scales rub against me I dunk my head
& see you Maxime turn into a jellyfish
Saint Christopher dangles from your neck
he's scraping against porcelain with his nails
& I don't know how bones get so heavy
a pair of lungs the island of Guadeloupe
stop absorbing water Maxime
the man from the hotline told me that if I say your name
again you won't taste how sweet the water has become
please stop opening your mouth
there's a fish in my bathtub he climbs into throats
scientists estimate he can live up to sixty years or more
they say he has ten eyes from which he spits blood
to scare off his predators
he's an endangered species Maxime please pull the cord
Maxime the crew is at my door I can hear them
I can't see anything past this

LET ME TELL YOU THE THINGS YOU ARE MISSING FROM

There's a cat that shows up in door frames each time he smells death.
He paws his way in. Tipsy, I ran into a shadow at my feet.

I'm getting stranded in my mouth when I see two knives go to love.
Here, I love you, accepting more suggestions.

2 am & another dies in terms of a low • sun.
Long ago we scratched in our sleep.

I've grown mortified by finality,
I mean that everything hides us. Look, trees.

THE BODY STANDS NO CHANCE

Day in & out I crave to attend weddings & funerals.
The ritual of white & velvet carries me further
than my own ceremonies.

Mornings & I leave for work & check to see
that the stove is off. I turn it back on to hear
the click followed by flame. I turn it off again. I turn it off.

I get in the elevator, a levitating coffin with vinyl ply
wood & a small dusted vent. The floor reeks
of soured milk & yet it takes everything in me to keep

myself from licking it. I stare passively at the reflection
of my face inside a round window. With each level, I am
decapitated & submerged in blackness followed by a burst

of light. I go down. In the subway platform I stand ground
on the delta, I allow space for fainting, for getting pushed,
for pushing, for jumping out, the sound of bone crushing.

What scares me most is not coming back to the dinner table,
to the couch, to my plants, to my pans, my books, my bed,
my cat, to the side of my beloved.

I shower with the clear shower curtain pulled away, with
the bathroom door open. I make eye contact with any stranger
with an agenda to break in & strangle me.

I consider growing out my nails to be ready to put up
the good fight. I know that it's important to be alert

around strangers & I know what beasts are capable of.
A headache is never just an ache. It's a mini stroke, a nosebleed,
a hemorrhage (that I mistake for a hemorrhoid). The times I drink too
much & self-diagnose myself with liver cancer. I'm suddenly hungry for pâté.

Summer in NYC & the rooms are swelling. I walk straight ahead
beneath hundreds of hazardously installed AC units. My headache
is definitely just a headache. If I'm still walking & it's been an hour, I'm not dying.

I measure happiness in knowing & with fingers, hunt my skin
for marks, for scars, my body keeps close to the source &
I dig into translucence till striking red.

The thought of being able to carry a poppy seed, a pepper corn,
a pomegranate seed, a small blueberry, or a cranberry bean, a cherry,
a kumquat, a Brussels sprout, a passionfruit, a Meyer lemon, a nectarine,

an apple, an avocado, a pear, a yam, a mango! A small artichoke
as long as a carrot, the size of a papaya, an eggplant, an ear of corn, or acorn
squash, a zucchini, a head of cauliflower, a kabocha or butternut squash,

a petite chou, a pineapple, a cantaloupe & rind, honeydew,
a swiss chard, a rhubarb, watermelon with umbilical cord,
all alarms me & leaves me full.

Being a martyr terrifies me. The thought of dislocating my knee,
dislocating my knee on the train, me dislocating the train
on the tracks with my knees bent.

I can handle myself in a room lit with fire. I quiet & crouch,
stalk shadows and coolness until I see an escape. I make my way back home, back
to my dinner, back to my cake & I'm fine. All the beasts are fed. Including me.

[MORE BLOOD IN THE EAST VILLAGE]   the laundromats continue

their coined cycle   I'll need more than just four hours to be saved

egg is French for bump   that closeness to having a belly full

of mirrors
                              & seeing you in Alphabet City this morning I sat

outside my face   so many pounds of us half out before me

(wishing my two little nephews a wonderful first snow)

days walk in my mouth   en route to my liver's hem

I sink night   lover to lover the greenness of small

suitcases & movings

the month of sun   I pick up wet leaves & press

them to my cheeks   the ground is cold   it's readying itself for us

I sat outside in a bathtub garden   planning trips instead of food

Frank   you're shooting me   you remain horizontal

I trade in stinkbugs   for   a whole almond

HOW MUCH WHISKEY AM I SUPPOSED TO DRINK BEFORE I BECOME A GHOST

I don't know
what it is with people
dropping before the winter.
I take the F train to East Village
where I sit on a bench
in Tompkins Square.
There's a woman with Leslie's eyes.
I've never met Leslie,
but the woman in the park
has her eyes & she's feeding
the plump black squirrels.
Maman doesn't register
on the donor list because
Dad doesn't want her eyes
to open on a different tree.
No one in America wants my mad blood,
no one in America wants my colon
blossoming pomegranate-sized tumors,
or my unfeminine uterus, unable
to carry an almond.
There must be manuals
on how to keep everything in.
How to stitch your lips together,
glue eyelashes closed for the wake.
But no matter how you scrub skin,
bone is bone is bone
& the smell of death,
the loss of pigment,
still lingers behind the ear.

RANDOM ATTACK

A shower curtain pretends to be a forest w/
bark painted on no birch exists

in Brooklyn no forests I plant
a universe of moss in a broken

light bulb add in plastic sheep &
their keeper I draw tarot cards

from Maman's palm knowing
she can't read her own blood

(my fortune goes unannounced)
after rain I go out to the streets

pick up snails let them slink
up & down my arms

I mistake my neighbor's
face on fire for the moon

LILY OF THE VALLEY

I.

All bulby & flushed white.
Sent on the first of May for G's Birthday.
Just a year ago I swore to oath her in silence
after I told her: "Your friend
who you saw yearly at weddings
& who visits you & your little family,
who you see at concerts & break
bread & spill egg yolks
over brunch with. Yes. Him.
He raped me."
A beat & the room goes mute.
"He raped me." A beat. Beat.
Me: "He raped me."
"He raped me?"
"G, can you hear me?"
G did & said she doesn't believe
it's a type of hunger
he is capable of.

II.

The Lily of the Valley delivered
to her home. It is a good home &
my nephews find the box covered in dirt.
A year in & I move to California.
There the dirt isn't laced
with chips of plates or lead paint.
There are snails & earthworms,
the occasional tiny beetle.
There the dirt is readying
itself & I box it up in vases.
Sometimes I plant an onion bulb
in mason jars. Give it
time, the bulb will shed
into stalk with a tower full
of tiny white bells.

III.

I'm moving back to New York City
to be closer to the Cathedral
of St. John the Divine where
I'll sprinkle Californian dirt
on the marbled altar with a carved baby
lamb all in gold. I've got too many oaths
to take & keep a small knife
in my boot. It's a hunger
G doesn't know.
Don't be mistaken:
I'm not one of the dead,
all fanning & white.

IV.

I lay out in velvet craned
above a porcelain bowl.
I've turned to purges
of dim sum & pork buns.
I'm all for eating tiny pillows
all stuffed & featherless.
My hunger has become relentless.
I file my teeth & keep them sharp,
they cut into cheek,
my tiny beets.
My hunger has gone bad.
My good sister doesn't believe
in such cravings. At night, in dark
I'll roam past each stoop & ironclad
doorway searching for that son.
That son of a bitch.
I'll press his head
to the ground & make him
sniff the dirt & dig,
his fingers dirty &
that son will be reading
himself a grave.

THE TWO MATRONS OF DEATH

Bound from church bells & funerals, Amelia & Delirium wear
their hair in a single, waist-length braid. They share a habit of mirroring:

when one's tooth hurts, the other bleeds from the gums,
when one's cunt blushes, the other tastes buttermilk all week.

Mornings are spent pricking their lips with bee stingers
& tying black ribbons to each other's underwear before going out

knocking coffin to coffin. They bend over to smell every mouth,
determining causes of death: black plague, weakened heart,

hookworm, polio & pus. They report their finding back to the reign. They retire,
wrists adorned with wreaths woven with dearly departed hair, plucked & knotted

into a fanning orchid. Desiring velvet, they eat pickled beets in bed. Amelia pretends
she is in the woods devouring the heart of a lamb. Delirium adds a bit of sugar.

HONEY BADGER

It's been a long winter, drunk
from stripping away root &
bulb of berries. I know twelve ways

to be avoided & watch snakes weave
into sand, cracked lightning bolts,
their rattles burst night open.

Khrya ya ya ya Khrya ya ya ya

Then comes the spring to kill. It makes
me dizzy, how blood rushes to the surface
and paints everything ruby throated,

torn ligaments flossing in between
my canines. Sweetness ends
with my nose in the front door of a house

full of bees. I claw my way in, split
the walls, nails dripping in gold honey.
What's a swarm of stings?

The bees form three masks for birthday
wishes around their intruder. I open my mouth,
invite them in, just to get the smell of me.

CALVARY

I ride naked on a crystal elephant to the gates of dawn,
the priests pierced my nipples with the corners of a golden crucifix.
I'm your savior, your mother.

I want you to bite me here,
pull the raspberries away
until skin tears.

At the center of town square I dismount
my elephant & crouch with a paintbrush
in my cunt & paint.

Priests wrap halfmoon's crescent
around my neck & watch as brushstrokes get heavier.
They want me to lick myself off

the floor, bleed so their stars
have something dark to shine in.
You'll have to break me

before putting me in the ground with flecks
of gold paint on my thighs. My arm not worthy
of being a relic nailed to the walls of your cathedrals,

my teeth not white enough to be encased in a green amber ring, the eyes
of a cat left without milk. No femur of mine holy & framed
in a silver window of your breast.

SELF PORTRAIT AS BEAST INSIDE BELLY

7 months & Maman remained horizontal, wanting to stay close to dirt
while I floated among placenta & yolk sac.
Born with a crown of black hair, my namesakes:

Inès de La Fressange: an aristocrat turned model turned cokehead & fur clad
w/ a strand of hair on the tongue.

Inès the great-grand-aunt: who lived among trees sharpening her teeth on wolf bone.
She skinned a whole house out of their fur.

I've inherited:
A goat as a descent from stubbornness
A fondness for red
yolks & bread
neglect for the arm of illness
that tic of lifting my skirt
to see what I forgot.

A NEW FRONTIER

A tiny black-and-white cattle dog runs alongside
the plane, chasing down a Canadian goose.
He's legendary in Michigan, and for the split second
when the space between my vertebrae clenched
and loosened and we hit pavement, and we hit it hard,
I thought it was you incarnated to dog. I would have
guessed a monkey, a jaguar, an iguana,
but never a sheep herder. He catches the goose
before its neck and feet twist into propeller,
its body a union of feather and metal gears.
A man who taught me to write told me that I
was the type of woman to laugh in the throat
of death, I could kill by just looking at him.
Feral and all, he told me I was what a woman
should smell like. Could he smell the blood between my legs
caked on the sides as I always forgot to change the pad?
Let's be honest, I enjoyed bright turning rust.
I still love blood in snow. It turns me on.
Unlike my pad, the snow holds it in place,
the air too cold to turn it into anything.
Maman trained me to turn a key into a weapon and X-ed
all the spots that would take a man down to his knees.
I was presented with rape as *when* rather than *if.*
This new frontier is a littered landscape of hacked-off
nipples, the lips of cunts soft as apricots and left rotting
under polished boots. Nothing can save us from violence.
Unlike you, I don't ache to have children.
They terrify me. They could rape or be raped or die
and then what? What do you do when you produce something

that's broken and can't absorb it back into your being until
it's healed? I lined my legs with pellets of honey. No bees stung.
Nothing happened because I was the poacher. Guard down,
out I went to the woods with a hunter. He wore a suede coat
with fringes and turquoise beads, an inheritance of pipe smoke and cologne.
He promised to take me to see a dead deer, eyes black with flies,
sprawled out and belly hacked. I thought it could be you,
so we trudged in knee-high snow. My nose dripped red dots
along the trail. White on white is dizzying
and I confused the sky for ground, both heavy from holding
the bones of the dead. I trailed behind the tanned suede skin,
further into the woods, and suddenly realized the space
missing between my legs. My weight collapses the burrowed
tunnels of squirrels. The hunter brings me to a circle of logs
where you weren't there. No deer, no organs split out and held by snow,
no flies or pus. Blood marking my face ugly, No Trespassing.
His hand smears red across my cheek, trying to forage
blush he presses it further in then turns to set down the suede
coat. For a second, the wind swept into the sleeve and the deer
that was promised was there. He dragged me closer to it,
all the wind had been knocked out. How heavy his hand
rests on my shoulder, I pissed myself a little.
Unarmed, I felt the weight of the falling snow. The hunter tells
me that my eyes are turning. Ten years out, I come
with green eyes, when raped my eyes are large and hazel
for days afterwards. The hunter pulls my hand to his pulse.
I can only hear mine. I wonder if he can smell my fear.
Is this what makes me more of a woman?
Does this make him crave honey and blood?
Here I am presenting my throat to the hunter, the peeled
skin of you, a deer waiting for my own blood to spill. I look down
at my own makeshift trail of blood and run back, back to the main
road. I hear the hunter yelling to stop. He wants me.
Later the hunter sits beside me, where I've built myself a fire,

my hands don't warm. Our bodies are meant to keep close to the source.
I'm too young to understand that it's just begun.
There will be others who don't promise me a deer, who don't
promise to be gentle, who don't promise the moon
or leave a mark for belief even after I say no.
There will be other hunters and they will be thirstier,
and they will push me down in a bed of snow, in a bed of sheets,
in a bed of wooden floor boards and pallets. I will wake in winter after
a ten-year sleep and find myself with legs bent and broken, my stomach intact
but my cunt ripped open and bleeding, a river as large as the Mississippi.
My eyes turned balls of black flies. The bed doesn't let me sink
further into the ground to join the other bones to be later dug
up by a black-and-white beast. Here my bones are pierced with light.
My head facing you, a hawk   circling.

E.V.

4 am & all the windows are yawning,
the baby pigeons remain hidden.
& my radio is a hummingbird,
there's no more honey left
when it announces the head
still missing of that
pregnant woman in Queens,
stabbed with a kitchen knife
her husband held.
I open the freezer
& find Leslie's sleeping mask.
Summer pushes my head further
in, beside a bag of frozen figs,
a grapefruit, popsicles.
No one will get this close w/o
crawling inside, making
a shed out of you.

THE SWALLOWS

The cathedral's coffin-carved
doors remain parted. Our Lady
with hands cupped upward
welcomes the masses, knee
to marble, arms heavy with Mary
& sorrow to a chalk Christ.
I light waxed wicks.
Along the Juárez border,
hundreds of pink crucifixes gather.
A pregnant Chihuahua drags
its tits across the pavement,
her little intestines moving.

NORDIC ART

(I paint eyes onto my nipples   light my hair on fire
to smell like burnt rice)
my love sleeps with her window open

there are no fireflies past   Amsterdam + 110
(I keep my window closed)
check to see the gas stove is off
turn the lock
check to see the gas stove is on
                            off
                        on
there's no more fire

there's a man on the 3
speaking with the devil
his tongue isn't split in two
a cobra head fanged   dangling
from his neck
(tells me he wants to baptize
his hands deep inside my mouth
I forget to breathe)

I'm twelve again
asleep in a room of mirrors
Maman paints red
on my palms
to dirty the face
of the beekeeper

EVERYTHING HIDES US

Shadows of fiddleheads fainting & the burst that follows.
Hands glowing in the dark, taking out light.

The possibility of fire erasing a face frightens me.
The remains of martyrdom: a teal car & a relic heart.

No more no more no more missing the smell of you.
Can't I crave something else today?

I'm blown away by the amount of cake served at funerals.
Promise you'll take care of me.

I've dislocated my own skin. We can't help
ourselves. We're that breakable.

April is almost here with her two versions of weather.
Bring less clothing, more hours.

THE MELLIFIED MEN

There is a tribe of martyrs who are fed honey,
nothing but raw gold for months.
Their jaws sink into combs until their teeth grow
twice the size, coated in wax.
Bathe them in honey
their toenails turn pollen.
Go ahead, you can kiss these feet.
Watch the skin loosen
from bones, too sweet
for its own marrow and how easily
it pulls apart. Their kidneys
churn out pellets of nectar
in place of urine, and soon
they're knees to chest
in a small wooden box,
dated with death
and buried in shallow
graves for a few hundred years
and then they will taste sweet
to the tongue and they
will be confection
and taken for remedy,
a looming ache above
the eyes, a bout of bruises
and the seasonal cold.
Imagine, a gold finger wrapped
and dangling on the neck
of a child to cure
a swollen tooth.

IN GOOD FAITH

Ona,   Good morning, love. Spent it eating apricots straight off the branches with Jamie. Dreamt about Leslie, she had no hands yet managed to set her mattress on fire.   Still haven't opened the tarot pack you got me.

Here the figs taste good, here we eat directly from trees.   Took the train to San Francisco for drinks w/my friend the Indian Prince. He shaved his head to give up sin. He writes letters posing as Zooey Blood   & writes to her mother saying he's sorry he can't attend the funeral.

On my walk back to the apartment   on Twin Peaks, a man pointed to my knee still in brace

& said *You've fucked too much in your previous life.* What about now?   Maybe I was a dog? That would explain my tongue.

Stood night up. Blue is the only hue I taste here.   *Blue of sky depends on the darkness of the empty space behind it   in which case blue is something of an ecstatic accident produced by void   & fire.* When we have a kitchen together, let's paint the walls with robin eggs.

Got lost for hours with Jamie while cruising   for strawberries. We squatted in bushes & peed, thinking we were alone, laughing as we looked out for snakes. Heard footsteps & found a brown cow standing a few feet from me,   her bell ringing. Peed   all over my skirt.

Missed your call & replayed your message.   I howled at the moon &   with it came an echo of coyotes. Here   people sleep nursing their guns, the doors   unlocked.

Here, we eat fireflies   straight off branches. Here, we tuck glow-in-the-dark Virgins in our pockets   & recite prayers by counting teeth.

BREAKING WINTER

FADE IN

(Girl is asleep in Leslie's red room. She stirs a bit & suddenly opens her eyes to the Beekeeper, who appears at the foot of her bed. She sits up. Beekeeper brings his finger to his veil & makes a hushing sound. Girl brings legs up to chest)

BEEKEEPER   GIRL

You're here.

(Beekeeper turns her nightstand light on)

What's happened to your face?

Why are you back?

I've missed you. It's been a while. Now, your face...

I tried to give it up & put it on someone else.

But no one wanted it?

(Girl buries her face in the sea of sheets)

& Leslie. Where is she?

(He looks around the apartment)

She's not here. Her mattress caught fire.
They took her away when she cut off her own hands.

& Wolf, where is he?

All he wants is meat now.

& you?

Just give me night & leave.

Open your mouth. Show me your teeth.

(Girl scoots to the end of the bed, holding the blanket close.
Beekeeper moves closer & holds her jaw, examining the front
teeth, his hands remain gloved)

Wider, open wider!

       (Girl hesitates)

Don't worry, this won't take long.
There are no bees to sting you.

                                                     Please, stop. I need my teeth.

(He tucks her in bed, his veil hovering over her
as he kisses her forehead)

FADE TO

(Girl wakes to winter. The room has been painted lavender.
Sticking out her tongue, she finds a small honeycomb. Girl
walks to the sink & pours salt on her tongue. Yet all she can
taste is honey. She crawls out of the window & sits on the fire
escape. Girl looks down to find a strand of teeth strung around
her neck. A thin layer of gum, pink, still embedded in its root.
Girl scratches it off. Blackbird appears perched on the ladder
& stares at her)

BLACKBIRD

Night open wide.
Night open wide.
Night open wide.

(Girl doesn't notice the shadow of Wolf at her feet)

YOUNG GIRL EATING A BIRD

This is not dinner   this is winter

                a girl holding a blackbird

this is a bird who does not chirp

this is how a young girl preys
neck bent cage broken open & tiny ribs slivering a piece of the moon

This is how she collects bird wings   & makes a crown of them

This is how a young girl makes herself full

PATRON SAINT OF ALL LOST THINGS

True I write letters to Leslie
snow on every leaf of Tompkins Park
she's a still death in New Jersey among tooth-shaped tombs
does dirt taste like beets
I stand up earl-grey late as white peels away my ceiling
the dead are always where you place them
& she doesn't write back so I have low expectations
when I open my mailbox the moon is blue
meow I am home
meow I am not here
Brooklyn & all the trees are on fire

I want to strike a match across my teeth & light
the kitchen on fire because the stove
is broken & has miscarried countless loaves
what else do I need but a glow-in-the-dark
Lady Guadalupe & my first paper tooth
tucked in the back pocket of my jeans

An autumn of Gingko fruit small & rotten
marks another year since Leslie's death beneath a ceiling
stuck on glow-in-the-dark stars & the navel
of the universe still is clogged from grayed roots
& cigarette-blessed gypsy moths
their wings opening breaths of accordions I'm going to leave you
& I'm not sorry

I fucked a man the last time
someone stepped on his grave
there's no lightning to crack open night

There's a man on the train who doesn't look anything
like my father & I want to kiss his eyelids
tonight because I cannot carry a piece of him
I eat spoiled fish in hopes of a belly full of tapeworms
& maybe I'll stop feeling so lonely

Please Leslie stop ripping my teeth out of me
when I look in the mirror all that's left
are canines please stop spinning
them like dreidels

Cut along the dotted lines
& leave me gutted skin to the touch
make the cut a sharp one because I've
given up on prey patchouli oil burnt wicks & dust
my knees are bruised I string beetle wings
in my hair & let it grow

Another person threw themselves on the tracks
Leslie's the one who wears a beekeeper's veil
the dead shall be raised

Forgive melanoma with all four of its syllables
& how the word grazed her skin away from him
forgive me love for I have sinned
& fallen over the hem for another man on the train
there will always be a name following yours
bend down & dig with your hands

Take my tongue but not my sight
I haven't looked up at the moon
in weeks but overheard on the radio
that scientists discovered a planet made from granite & diamonds
it's five times the size of earth
this year the bees have grown
plump & tired all the honey is spoiled with sea salt

Bless Maman who celebrates her fifty-seventh birthday
squatting in the bushes
bless the nine-year-old who walked from Mexico
to California with his palm sliced open
from a shattered mirror
bless the woman in Oaxaca she keeps the refrigerator open
& lets meat rot
bless the girl who spends morning leafing
an artichoke for truth

Hong Kong left me broke & horny
all that ping-pong during the monsoon season
the murmuring of motorcycles between my legs
the pork & chive dumplings
red bean paste or simply that fucking reverse
cow-girl meant I wouldn't have to look at him

He is gone
he is at the foot of your bed waiting to be undone
waiting for Leslie to draw him a hot bath

I sleep with a machete tucked beneath my pillow talk
to me when I dream & I will tell you who gave birth
to the moon she was fourteen wore a cape
in a forest of mirrors & ate berries while looking for black bears
to cut up to crawl inside their bellies until winter
broke this is how close I want you to get to me

If Maman drops her spoon on the floor
then the mice will give her a fork
if she dresses up as a small black bear
then the forest will burn until solstice
if you break the beehive in half
then your tongue will turn to marble

Praise the woman way down south at one hundred & five
she has lost her eyes ears & teeth but never forgets to cross herself
in Creole blessing her children with all of her tongue
praise the bats trapped in the walls their wings beating
in parallel to dream reels
praise the sphere hanging above the namesake
praise your lover who spun needles against Black Orpheus
the only record she didn't break when she found
your love always shared
I fuck in a room of mirrors
praise abuela who keeps fidelity
measured in rat poison tucked in jars with spices of confession
dried jalapenos she says to trust only a woman's hands
there's nothing left to be done but melt all the spoons

Forgive the man too eager to peel into gray of thighs
to even ask if I was thirsty for him

Forgive the hunter who only eats the meat he kills
he offers me his hands & knows they're not enough
I bite into the heart of a deer   it's winter

Rattlesnakes shed their skin across desert floor
in morning Maman smooths out the waves
their bodies left behind & she reads the weather
for the year

Is it a nice fall
I dress warm & go out into night where there are black bears
Maman put me on the bus to Brooklyn
it's almost spring but the earth remains frozen
too brick to break ground with shovel
I'm not dead just yet
Maman calls to tell me to rub cinnamon
behind my ears before I fall asleep

Are you afraid of bees
I've blistered the roof of my mouth with a spoonful of rice
but the bees don't sting this time of year
here it is changeable
each time I pass a laundromat in Harlem
scented soap brings my ear closer to Mexico
but the rest of me stays a rosebud
heavy from cinnamon-spiced whiskey & Coca-Cola
I spend morning throwing up in a toilet bowl

Red paint doesn't come off easily & so
I scratch skin away with fingernails
he can keep my dream reels of plucked
teeth-stained underwear parasites & anal
sex with all three of his brothers & avant-garde
theater director turned father

Maman won't forget me & even half around the world
she chants my name not hearing my teeth unzip pants
my father tells me to never give too much of myself away
I pluck strands of hair & hide them in pockets
& shoes it's afternoon & I knit a small nest
of sparrow in my hair
I wear white collared shirts without pants
& crawl around the bedroom meowing in all the corners

A bullet snagged my grandmother's right eye in Algeria
her head too heavy her left eye didn't blink
as my grandfather cleaned the gun
before tucking it in the front of his pants
did her jaw rattle did her teeth
split in two
the bullet grazed marrow
she smelled of orange peels
when they found her in a ditch with a holy crown of puzzle pieces
in her hair & her fingers were bathed in rose water
her feet pressed together & her body a cocooned
inferno & femur fossilized in an amber ring
she left behind two girls with pale skin who shared
a yellow room & who smell death behind their ears
when they sleep

How forgetful the dead can be during winter
knowledge like heat rises so my father
takes down our roof Maman hammers mirrors
into her own constellations
small fragments of reflections
leg arm & eyes
nothing else in the house left
to be broken cuts her thigh
the day after my death
a feather-tufted canary chirps
in the ears of every lover I've had

A small bus in Cusco packed
with Quechua men & women
on the way from Pisac to Chinchero
tumbles forty feet down a cliff after
the brakes give out
the sole survivor
a boy named Hatsu bird of the Andes
is trapped beneath the body of his abuelita
his lips painted with gold dust

A woman in Lyon wakes up after lying
in bed since the drowning of her son
she walks to the bathroom & cuts
threads of hair with rusted scissors
before setting them down on the sink
her husband sweeps the hair & clumps a small nest

There are two Inèses at the MoMA they're not part of the still life
nor the abstract exhibition they walk around naked
no flash please the skin doesn't take to such light
the one on the right has sliced off her breast
so she can write better & in its hollowness
is a beehive to sweeten breast milk
tilt your head back for her dancing black bears
the bees murmur at night
she doesn't dream
you will notice that the Inès on the left
has her face covered in flour & the far corners
of her eyes are in bedrooms painted gold where
it's always autumn & her tongue a cobra head
slashing her inner cheek
she spoils the milk while sitting
on the roof of city hall
reading tarot for the handless

SINKING CATHEDRAL

All the women in my family are buried here. Laid out facing west.
Of blood & bone, we hunger to haunt the living with grief & scare everyone white.

A sea of linen to mix along with gasoline until nothing is left
but architecture of bones. Caged, we miss the smell of rose on fingernails.

It's quiet down here & the heat is bearable. Cracked in two.
They've butchered you. A rib & femur pressed against dirt like a flower.

I rotate south & begin another year as a sacrificial
lamb with palms out. Let's consider

what the beekeeper is promising me
other than the front steps of the dead.

THANK YOU

Jim Daniels, you took a chance on me when no one knew what to do with me. Thanks to you, I was able to attend Carnegie Mellon and pursue my love for writing at the next level. You were patient and kind, and never took my admiration for granted. You devoted your life to your students, and it has not gone unnoticed. Keep at it.

Eileen Myles, you sparked something deep inside me while I was in your craft course while attending NYU's MFA program. You introduced me to a whole new school of writers and fostered me to write this manuscript. Your support encouraged me to be more daring in form and explore aspects of my voice I had no idea existed.

Thank you Geoffrey Nutter for creating Wallson Glass, you created a space for me to start writing after years of writing anxiety post MFA. Your encouragement to be playful in my writing allowed me to find myself back to the craft.

Many thanks to Wah Mohn for sharing his memories of his late mother, Leslie Mohn, who the long poem is dedicated to.

Many thanks to Genevieve and Phillip Genin for sharing memories of their son, my sweet friend Maxime Genin.

Erin Elizabeth Smith and Anna L. Black from Sundress Press for believing in my manuscript and helping me bring it into the world as a book.

To my friends Emily Nagin, Adele Barclay, Elise Nagy, and Madeleine Barnes for taking time to read through this manuscript in different iterations listen to late night ramblings, and provided crucial feedback, laughs, and have all encouraged me to keep writing.

Marci Calabretta Cancio-Bello, dear friend and exceptional editor throughout the years, first reading poems of mine while at Carnegie to now working on bringing to light, *Something Dark to Shine In*.

Bele and Maman, you believed in my ability to write at a very young age and saved my life by sending me to Interlochen, where I continued to grow as the writer I am today. You have never doubted my love for the craft, and have been my fiercest fans since that very first reading in a small coffee shop basement. Without your devotion to have me live my dreams, I would not be here. I am forever grateful for your love and nurture.

Ona, my love, there is no way I can write down all the support and love you've given me over the years. We met as two young poets eating pastries at The Hungarian Pastry Shop and reading poems on the train from Harlem to Park Slope. You patiently stood by my side as I tried to turn this manuscript into a reality, moving from West Coast to East Coast, and you never let me stop believing in myself as a writer. You're my first and favorite reader and editor. Forever your Honey Badger.

ABOUT THE AUTHOR

Inès Pujos holds an MFA in Poetry from NYU and lives in NYC. Her poems have appeared in *The Offing, Nightblock, The Journal, Fog Machine, Salt Hill Press, Poor Claudia, Cosmonauts Ave, Powder Keg, The Adroit Journal, Day One, Bone Bouquet, Cimarron Review, Gulf Coast, Phantom, Hayden's Ferry, Puerto del Sol,* and *Verse Daily,* among others. You can follow them at: inespujoscreative.com.

OTHER SUNDRESS TITLES

Cosmobiological
Jilly Dreadful
$20

Slaughter the One Bird
Kmbery nn Priest
$12.99

Dad Jokes From Late in the Patriarchy
Amorak Huey
$12.99

The Valley
Esteban Rodriguez
$12.99

What Nothing
Anna Meister
$12.99

To Everything There Is
Donna Vorreyer
$12.99

Hood Criatura
féi hernandez
$12.99

nightsong
Ever Jones
$12.99

I Am Here to Make Friends
Robert Long Foreman
$14.99

Maps of Injury
Chera Hammons
$12.99

JAW
Albert Abonado
$12.99

The Familiar Wild
$14.99

Lessons in Breathing Underwater
H.K. Hummel
$12.99

Bury Me in Thunder
syan jay
$12.99

Dead Man's Float
Ruth Foley
$12.99

Gender Flytrap
Zoë Estelle Hitzel
$12.99

Blood Stripes
Aaron Graham
$12.99

Boom Box
Amorak Huey
$12.99

Arabilis
Leah Silvieus
$12.99

Afakasi | Half-Caste
Hali F. Sofala-Jones
$12.99

Match Cut
Letitia Trent
$12.99

Marvels
MR Sheffield
$16.99

Passing Through Humansville
Karen Craigo
$12.99

Divining Bones
Charlie Bondhus
$12.99

www.ingramcontent.com/pod-product-compliance
Lightning Source LLC
Chambersburg PA
CBHW081238090426
42738CB00016B/3345